Basketball
A Family Affair

by Coach Wes Shepard

Coach Shepard brings a wealth of doing basketball, GOD'S WAY! There are two ways of doing everything – even basketball: Man's way and God's way. Coach Shepard doesn't disconnect basketball from God. In a day and age when so many youngsters and parents are told that faith in Christ should not mix with athletics, academics and attitudes, Coach Shepard's *Basketball: A Family Affair* is a breath of fresh air as he interweaves biblical principles into the teaching of basketball fundamentals.

Colossians 3:17 says, "whatsoever you do in word or deed, do all in the name of the Lord Jesus Christ." Coach Shepard knows that includes basketball.

If you want to know how to do basketball in the name of Jesus Christ this book is for you.

Ron Brown
State Director
Fellowship of Christian Athletes-Nebraska

I congratulate Dr. Shepard for his coaching accomplishments over the past 50 years and being selected for the Nebraska and National High School Athletic Coaches Association Hall of Fame.

His faithfulness in teaching the fundamentals of basketball and of life to thousands of young people has been multiplied many times in lives across the country.

John Hammond
Vice President of Basketball Operations
Detroit Pistons

The Fellowship of Christian Athletes is touching millions of lives ... one heart at a time. Since 1954, the Fellowship of Christian Athletes has been challenging coaches and athletes on the professional, college, high school, junior high and youth levels to use the powerful medium of athletics to impact the world for Jesus Christ. FCA is the largest Christian sports ministry in America. FCA focuses on serving local communities by equipping, empowering and encouraging people to make a difference for Christ.

VISION
To see the world impacted for Jesus Christ
through the influence of athletes and coaches.

MISSION
To present to athletes and coaches and all whom they influence the challenge and adventure of receiving Jesus Christ as Savior and Lord, serving Him in their relationships
and in the fellowship of the church.

MINISTRIES
The FCA Ministries encourage, equip and empower coaches and athletes on the professional, college, high school, junior high and youth levels to use the powerful medium of sports to
impact their world for Jesus Christ.

The FCA Ministries are:
Coaches
Campus
Camp
Community

Jesus answered and said to him, "Truly, truly, I say to you, unless one is born again, he cannot see the kingdom of God."
John 3:3

Dedicated to

Rose

*a coach's very special wife
and mother of three sons,
formerly successful coaches,
– Greg, Mark, and Scott –
who have joined their sister,
Denise, as outstanding school
administrators, and with their
wives, Kelly, Kim and Heather,
and husband, Eric, have
blessed us with sixteen
grandchildren.*

*Appreciation is also expressed
to all the coaches and players
I have been privileged
to work with over 50 years.
Thanks to all of you.*

Wes Shepard

A note of thanks to Larry Porter,
who edited the copy; Ili Lefler,
for the layout; photographer
Frank Staskiewicz and the players
who demonstrated the skills.

Copyright © Wes Shepard
Publisher: Cross Training Publishing
ISBN: 1-929478-74-7
For additional copies:
Cross Training Publishing
PO Box 1874
Kearney, NE 68848
800-430-8588
www.crosstrainingpublishing.com

A Challenge From the Coach

> King Solomon wrote in **Proverbs 22:6,** it is the parents' responsibility to "Train up a child in the way he should go; even when he is old he will not depart from it."

As a teacher and coach, I realized that many parents are not as actively involved in their children's school experiences as they would like to be. I have always encouraged parents to attend conferences, camps, clinics and activities and given them opportunities to ask questions and voice concerns about their children.

This handbook is for parents who want to teach their son or daughter basketball skills on the driveway, coach a team for the "Y" league or just enjoy the game more as a spectator.

Athletic competition provides life experiences that are rewarding to the athlete and his or her parents and that will mold lives pleasing to God and to others they influence.

Jesus said, "I have come that they might have life and have it abundantly." **John 10:10**

Jesus Christ is God. He came to earth to demonstrate that life can be lived to the fullest without violating God's laws. He is the model of a perfect life in a world that rejected Him. Yet He humbled Himself, remained obedient to His Father, even suffered death on a cross, and was raised back to life three days later in order to pay the penalty for our disobedience to God (committing sin). In this demonstration of God's love, Jesus made it possible for us to have a personal relationship with Him that assures us of eternal life with Him in heaven.

It is my prayer that this book will be meaningful to you parents as well as to your son or daughter.

In His love,
Coach Shepard

Parents' Role

- Parents are to be encouragers. They must accept responsibility for their child's academic, athletic, moral and spiritual development.
- A commitment to excellence is asked of everyone.
- Communication during the season is essential.
- Parents' attendance at all student activities is important.
- Parents should provide a positive role model for their children.
- The coach needs to provide a clear understanding of the program to athletes and their parents.
- Be a good testimony to the Lord in your home, on the basketball court and in the stands.

Basketball is a tough game and players must be in excellent physical condition not only to perform at their best but to help avoid injuries. Not many games are as strenuous as basketball because of the emphasis placed on constant movement – quick stops and starts, sudden changes in direction, running and falling on a hardwood floor.

Parents need to let the coach do his job and be willing to assist in any way they can.

"And, fathers, do not provoke your children to anger, but bring them up in the discipline and instruction of the Lord."
Ephesians 6:4

Table of Contents

Goals & Commitments 8

Knowledge & Leadership 10

Shooting 12

Player's Personal Shooting Plan 17

Passing 18

Dribbling 21

Rebounding 22

Screening 24

Penetrating 24

Offensive Player Positions 26

Primary Fast Break 28

Secondary Fast Break 30

Motion Offense 32

Defense 36

Commitment 42

About the Author 46

Fellowship of Christian Athletes 47

Basketball Terminology & Symbols 48

References 50

Goal 1. To develop the following character qualities through commitment.

Goal 2. To assist athletes in understanding and making solid commitments consistent with Scripture.

Commitments

1. To God First
"You shall love the Lord your God with all your heart and with all your soul and with all your mind." **Matthew 23:37**

2. To Your Family
"Let your father and mother be proud of you; give your mother happiness." **Proverbs 16:20**

3. To Your Church
"Let us consider how to stimulate one another in love and good deeds, not forsaking our own assembling together." **Hebrews 10:24, 25**

4. To Your School
"To whom much is given, of him much is required; the man to whom much more is given, of him much more is required." **Luke 12:48**

5. To Your Team
"Now the body is not made of one part but of many so that there should be no division in the body, but that its parts should have equal concern for each other. If one part suffers, every part suffers with it; if one part is honored, every part rejoices with it." **1 Corinthians 12:14, 25, 26**

Goals and Commitments

6. To Set an Example
"But if anyone causes one of these little ones who believes in me to sin it would be better for him to have a large millstone hung around his neck and to be drowned in the depths of the sea."
Matthew 18:6, 7

7. To Do Your Best
"He who sows sparingly shall also reap sparingly, and he who sows bountifully shall also reap bountifully."
2 Corinthians 9:6

8. To Persevere
"We also rejoice in our trials, knowing that trials bring about perseverance; and perseverance, proven character; and proven character, hope; and hope does not disappoint." **Romans 5:3-5**

9. To Play by the Rules
"If anyone competes as an athlete, he does not receive the victor's crown unless he competes according to the rules."
2 Timothy 4:12

10. To Be a Winner
"Do you not know that in a race all runners run, but only one wins the prize? Run in such a way as to win the prize. Everyone who competes in the games goes into strict training. They do it to win a crown that will not last, but we do it to win a crown that will last forever."
1 Corinthians 9:24, 25

Knowledge & Leadership

- Study the game plan, fully understand it and commit your efforts to making it happen. See the moves of your teammates and opponents.

- Each part of the game is important. The pre-game preparation by the coach and players is key to top performance. Your attitude en route to the gym, in the locker room and during warm-up on the floor will dictate your success. Enthusiasm, concentration and execution is the theme.

- Be sure that your team wins on the inside of the court and keeps its opponents honest on the perimeter, taking advantage of the strengths of each player on your team. The most productive play on offense is to draw a foul as you take the ball to the basket and score.

- When penetrating the defense, perimeter players must be willing to pull up and shoot, dump the ball to a teammate or back out when a trap develops.

- Good ball and player movement results in point production. Be poised and confident; don't try to force passes, shots and drives. Play within your ability.

- You are in charge when you have the ball. Don't be afraid to make a mistake. When a teammate errs, pick him up and acknowledge him for good play.

Practice!!!

Practice! Practice! Practice!

- You should love to practice, and you should seek to develop intensity, concentration and execution from the time you set your foot on the court until you leave.
    - a. Non-basketball talk leads to non-production.
    - b. Enthusiasm is a must throughout each practice.

- Be smart! Be dressed in uniform; put on your game face.

- As practice moves from drill to drill, you take the lead to get your teammates going.

- Getting tired or hurt is part of practices and games. Get up and get going; play harder.

- Defense takes commitment — 80% desire; 10% skill; 10% ability. Work hard and often!

- Never give less than your best, and know that you gave it all.

Shooting Hand Position

Elbows extended

Ball on fingertips

Eyes on target

Elbow bent

Weight on balls of feet

Set Shot

The traditional set shot includes facing the basket in a balanced position, with the shooter's arm in a U-shape directly above the knee, and the ball resting in a pocket formed in his hand. If he is right-handed, his right foot will be slightly forward and to the side of the left foot.

The shooter sights the basket over the ball, bends his knees and explodes upward, extending the arm up and towards the basket, following through with the hand and index finger dipping as though it is reaching into the basket.

Eyes on target

Elbow lined up to basket

Knees bent

Weight on balls of feet

Ball on fingertips

Head up

Feet spread squared on basket

Shooting

Jump Shot

The shooter squares up to the basket, feet parallel and knees bent. He raises the ball to the forehead, with the arm U-shaped and shooting hand holding the ball, until he reaches the height of the jump. The shooter sights the basket under the ball, extending his arm, and follows through, as in the set shot.

A player should be able to shoot effectively with either hand. When a dribbler drives left, he should shoot with the outside or left hand, unless guarded to his left. When driving right, the shot should be delivered with the right hand, unless guarded to the right. Lay-ups follow the same rule.

Statistics have also proved that when the shooter is at an angle on either side of the basket within two-point range, the ball should be shot at the backboard. This will result in a higher percentage of shots made.

The jump shot is designed to:
- Enable a player to attack the basket off the dribble, pass, and/or fake-and-go.
- Permit quick delivery of the ball to the basket.
- Allow the shooter to control the taller and stronger defensive player.
- Ensure a higher shooting percentage.

Right and Left Hand Lay-up

For young or inexperienced players, the lay-up is introduced in five steps:

1. Run a player without the ball to the right side of the basket, have him reach up with the right hand and climb with the right foot.
2. Second drill is the same as above with a ball and no dribble.
3. Third drill is with one dribble, long step and shot off the backboard, above the basket; add number of dribbles according to the length of the drive.
4. Use the same plan for shooting with the left hand.
5. To protect the ball, it is critical that the player shoots with the hand away from the defender.

An uncontested lay-up shot from either side of the basket should be an automatic two points. Many are missed because of lack of concentration, poor shooting habits or failure to establish the proper position under the board.

Ball on fingertips

Palm faces the board

Jump high to basket

Release ball at peak

Eyes on target

Shooting

The Power Shot

The power shot, or put-back, follows an offensive rebound or drive along the baseline with the rare. A shooter has his shoulders squared with the board and springs straight up as high as possible, shooting with the outside hand, and off the backboard.

Protect the ball with two hands

Release with outside hand

Jump high toward basket

Jump Shot/Free Throw Record

SHOOTING ROUTINE – Alternate hands on dribble and shot
Zone 1– 8-10 feet from basket; 1 dribble to basket
Zone 2 –10-14 feet from basket; 1 dribble to basket
Zone 3 – 15-20 feet from basket; 1 dribble to basket

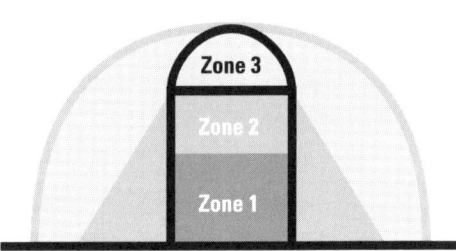

PLAN – Dribble toward basket left or right with outside hand; pick up ball; jump; turn in air; land on both feet squared to basket; explode up for jump shot with outside hand; angle shot off glass; follow to basket for rebound and second shot off glass, if missed; return to starting point for next shot.

GOALS – Complete 3 sets. On missed shot, rebound and power up on second shot; re-start count. Always begin shooting in Zone 1. After completing Zone 1, go to Zone 2, then Zone 3. Start with 5 straight made shots, and after completing successfully, expand to 10, 15, 20, 25. Shoot 10 free throws after each set.

Check out your shooting stance
- Position of your feet.
- Alignment – square your body.
- Gripping the ball – both hands.
- Position of ball – forehead (look under the ball).
- Focus – on board, basket.
- Jump and follow through, extend arm and hand; maintain balance.

A chart on the following page has been provided for you to record your results.

Zone 1	Zone 2	Zone 3	FT Shot	FT Made	Zone 1	Zone 2	Zone 3	FT Shot	FT Made	Zone 1	Zone 2	Zone 3	FT Shot	FT Made	Zone 1	Zone 2	Zone 3	FT Shot	FT Made

Passing

Passing is a major offensive weapon used by players to:

- Advance the ball quickly against an opponent's press.
- Outlet to a teammate by a defensive rebounder for a quick break down the floor.
- Get the ball to a cutter or center posted up in the lane.
- Reverse the ball away from a potential trap.
- Set up a scoring situation off the give-and-go.
- Skip pass to the other side of the court to a teammate who is open to shoot.
- Wisely control the time on the clock.

Floor awareness, body balance, reaction, timing and accuracy are critical factors in the passing game.

Passing/Receiving – Two-hand Chest Pass

PASSING
Head up
Flex elbows
Knees bent
Weight on balls of feet

RECEIVING
Spread hands
Keep eyes on ball
Flex elbows
Protect ball with arms and body

Passing

Bounce pass

- Head up
- Elbows extended
- Ball released off fingertips
- Knees bent
- Weight on balls of feet

Baseball pass

- Fingertip control
- Elbow points to receiver
- Body in balance
- Weight shifts to left leg

Overhead pass

- Head up
- Elbows extended
- Ball released off fingertips
- Weight on balls of feet

Hook pass

- Fingers spread
- Eyes on target
- Left arm protects
- Legs balanced

Dribbling

Each player needs to advance the ball up the court with either one or more passes to teamates, and/or by dribbling the ball.

The high dribble permits the athlete to explode after either a defensive rebound or pass reception so he can move rapidly full-court for a lay-up or pull-up jumper.

The low dribble is best when in heavy traffic or while protecting the ball from the defense. Use your off-hand and draw the ball closer inside to deny the defender the interception.

High dribble – for speed

Head up
Wrist and finger control
Good balance

Low dribble – for control

Arm out
Ball arm extended
Knees bent

Defensive Rebounding

When playing defense and your opponent is not in a position to receive the ball, open up and move toward the basket; get your body into the proper angle that you expect the ball to come, with feet wide, knees bent, arms extended and palms open to the basket.

Spot the ball on the board, and time your jump to catch and grip the ball in the air.

When you land, pivot to the outside and look for outlet players both on the sides and center.

Pass to outlet players, or dribble out hard to either side or middle with the dribbling hand away from the defender.

Eyes on the ball
Wide stance
Go for the ball

Rebounding

Boxing Out Your Opponent

When any player shoots, immediately turn and sprint toward the player for whom you are responsible. Pivot, so your back is close to him; widen your feet; bend both knees and bend your elbows shoulder-high, with arms extended and palms open to the basket.

Yell "Shot!" Then sprint into position for the rebound, unless ordered to drop back by your coach.

**Eyes on the ball
Elbows out, hands high
Block your opponent
Knees bent
Wide stance**

Offensive Rebounding

If you are on offense and your opponent is not in a position to go to the basket, look for an opportunity to flash to the ball. Otherwise, "Think Board." Get into position to rebound the ball, depending on the angle of the shot.

Expect the ball to come to you; plant and widen your feet with knees bent and arms extended with palms open to the basket.

Spot the ball on the board or basket; time your jump to catch and grip it in the air.

When you land, put it right back up for the put-back off the board. It is possible to tip it back in, provided you can jump high enough.

Screening

The purpose of the screen is to assist a teamate to get free from the defender when he is driving to the basket or advancing the ball up the floor.

The screen is also used to create an opportunity for a teammate to flash to a position where he can receive a pass and get a shot at the basket.

- A legal screen may be set for a teammate by a player moving close to a stationary position visible to the opponent, short of contact.

- If the opponent cannot see the screener, he must give the other player room for one step toward the screen without making contact.

- Neither player may use his hands or arms to prevent movement by the other.

Penetration

When squared up on the perimeter, a player may create a scoring situation by:

- Faking and dribbling into an open spot toward the basket, coming to a jump stop, springing up and shooting a jump shot (at the basket, if straight-away, or using the board, if at an angle).
- Fake left, crossover right and drive the baseline; slide into a squared position toward the basket, power up and shoot with the right hand off the board.
- Dribble to an open spot from the point, wing, or corner, with eyes toward the basket, and then pass to the center or baseline cutter.

Penetration/Movement Without the Ball

- Always shoot with the hand away from defender, whether inside or out, at the basket or board.
- A player may penetrate with or without the ball, using the V-cut and back-door cut, or flash.
- Dribble with the hand away from the defender, eluding him with special moves.
- With or without the dribble, use the give-and-go, split, back-door cut or screen, to or away from the ball at any time.

Player Movement Without the Ball

Every player should be taught how to move without the ball when attacking an opponent's defense

They need to have the ability to V-cut before coming to meet the pass on the perimeter, to be able to flash through the center lane or out on the perimeter and to cut along the baseline to create scoring opportunities for the team.

Players waiting for a pass flat-footed, gives the opponent an opportunity to intercept the ball.

The only exception should be for a center who is posted up wide momentarily in a position to receive the ball. He should jump to the pass to prevent an interception.

No. 1 The Point Guard

Each player has an important role to play, but the point guard is crucial to the success of the team. He is the most all-around skilled player. He possesses special leadership qualities and understands the coach's perspective of the game since he is the floor leader in games and practices.

- The point guard must maintain a positive attitude regardless of the score and must positively approach officials and opponents.
- He keeps the team together — starters and substitutes — and stops negative talk by teammates or anything else that might hurt morale.
- The point guard sparks the game tempo, creates scoring opportunities and serves as the floor leader on both ends.
- He keeps his eye on each player and the coach, continuously communicating with both.
- The point guard may be a major scorer, but his focus is to be on total team involvement, both offensively and defensively.

Nos. 2 and 3 Guards

These two players are very important. They are skilled in all areas and have similar leadership qualities as the point guard. They study the game, develop creativity in penetration, have quickness, possess unselfish attitudes and are willing to mix it up.

- Guards must be mobile. They must play either wing or the point. They must be able to flash to the post, screen and rebound.
- Each guard may start the offense or defense, depending on his spot on the floor during transition.
    a. On transition to offense, they may receive the outlet or second passes on the fast break, or a long pass on the fly.
    b. On defense, they set the tone by how they meet the player with the ball, utilizing intensity and pressure.
- If one off-guard moves to the No. 1 point guard spot, he must fill the role similar to what the first point guard had done.

Offensive Player Position

Nos. 2 and 3 Guards cont'd

- When in the No. 2 or No. 3 guard spots, he is expected to shoot, drive or create an opportunity for his teammates and know where each teammate is, being able to spot the center or flasher.
- On offense, the center or flasher must post up between his defender and the potential passer. He should demand the ball vocally, jump to the pass and look the ball into his hands. Then he should check the basket and either shoot, drive to the basket or pass to a teammate.

No. 4 Forward and No. 5 Center or Forward

The Nos. 4 and 5 players on the court are crucial to success for any team since they have a major responsibility to score and control the boards on both ends of the floor. This demands strength, quickness, stamina and a cool head. He must ignore extra physical pressure and go strong to the basket to score or rebound.

- Forwards are interchangeable and may play inside or outside. They are major power players on the team.
- They are rebounders – position minded, committed to rebounding and making the put-back shot.
- Inside players rebound, pass to outlet receivers and fly downcourt into position to score.
- On transition to defense, the forward or center may challenge his opponent with the ball or be first down to defend his basket. Play smart; don't get a cheap foul.
- On offense, post players flash in or post up on the defenders. They show the target, call "Ball," look the pass into their hands, drop a foot and focus on the basket. They then can go for a lay-up, pivot and shoot, or pass to a teammate and get into rebound position.

Primary Fast Break

A primary fast break takes place on turnovers, defensive rebounds and interceptions.

Transition from defense to offense may range from a single breakaway with no defenders to 2-on-0 or 3-on-0 situations, or 2-on-1, 3-on-1 or 3-on-2 breaks.

The goal is to beat the opponent to the basket for a lay-up or short jumper, with all offensive men up the court. The shooter and two others are to go for the rebound,

As a general rule, offensive players gain advantage by either outnumbering their opponent or creating a one-on-one situation, either inside or outside.

Offensive rebounders must learn to see the right angle on the board, get inside position on a defender, box out and time their jump with arms outstretched and eyes on the ball. Put back the ball if the shot is missed.

If this does not occur, or you do not get the basket, all five men are responsible to sprint back to the defensive area, unless pressing full court. But if you retain the ball, set up a secondary break or move into motion offense.

On the primary fast break, try to either pass the ball quickly up the court to a teammate who is breaking to the basket up the middle or dribble to the center of the court.

If five players are involved in the primary break, fill lanes 1, 3, and 5. Trailers are to fill lanes 2 and 4.

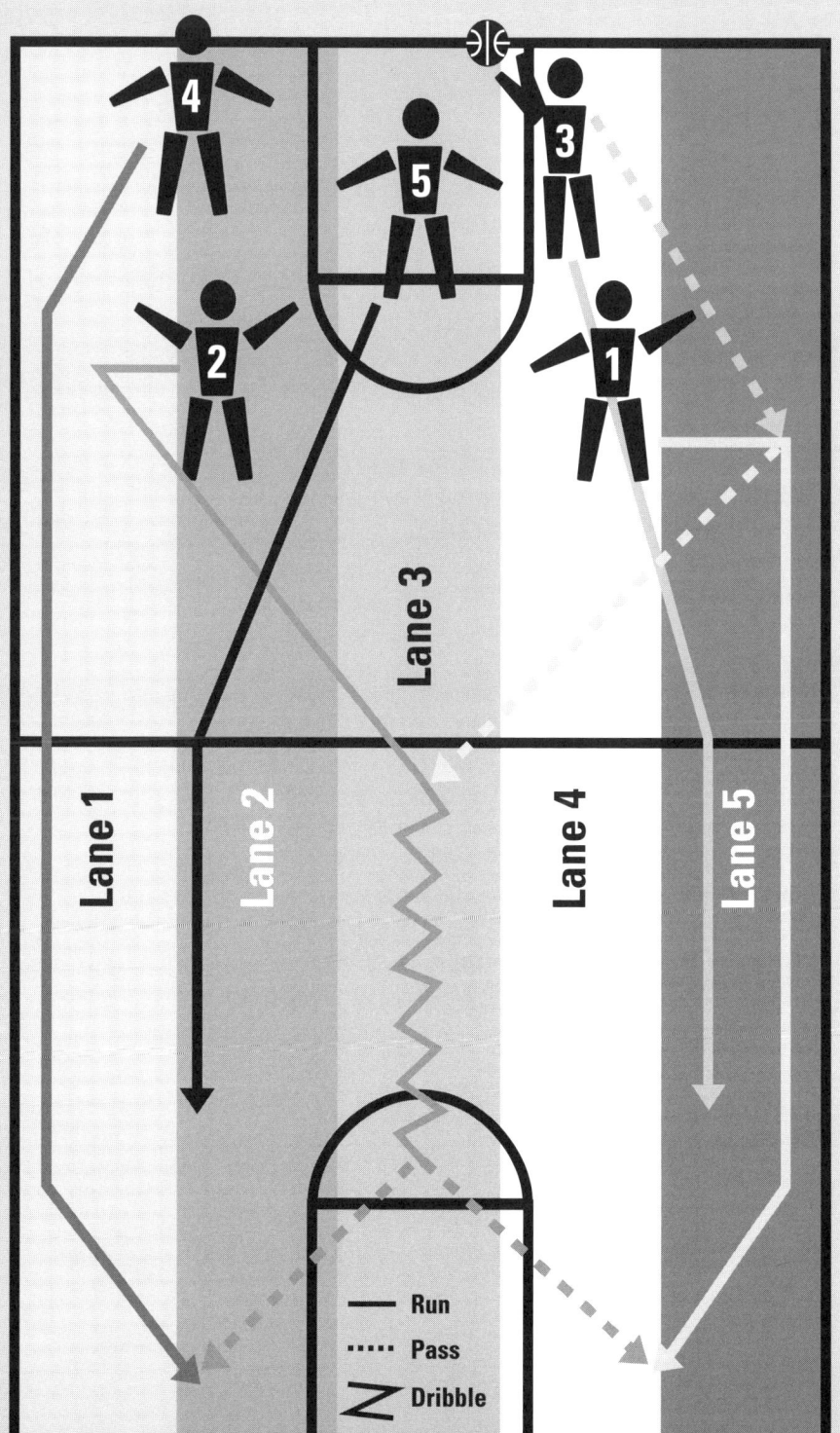

Secondary Fast Break

It is not always possible to get a primary fast break on transition. Then switch into a secondary break from either sideline or center.

The rebounder passes the ball to an outlet receiver – **G1** – who dribbles or passes to the center, looking for a primary break first.

G2, the second player downcourt, sprints to the ball-side corner, V-cuts, turns inside and looks for the pass from **G1**.

C5, the third player, sprints to the ball-side baseline block and posts up strong, calling for the ball and giving a target to the passer.

F4, the fourth player, sprints to the baseline block away from the ball, setting up for the rebound or curling inside the lane for the ball.

G3, the fifth player is the trailer. He stops at the top of the key, ball-side, and looks for a return pass or serves as a defender in case there is an interception.

G1 may penetrate, pass to **G2** on a give-go play, flash off a back pick by **C5**, move to an opposite corner for a skip pass or pass to **F4** or **C5** in the post.

G2 may penetrate, shoot, pass to **F4** or **C5** in the post or reverse the ball to **G3**.

G3 flashes to the ball if reversed by **G2**. He may then shoot, penetrate, pass to the post, skip pass to **G1** in the opposite corner or dribble to the key to start motion offense.

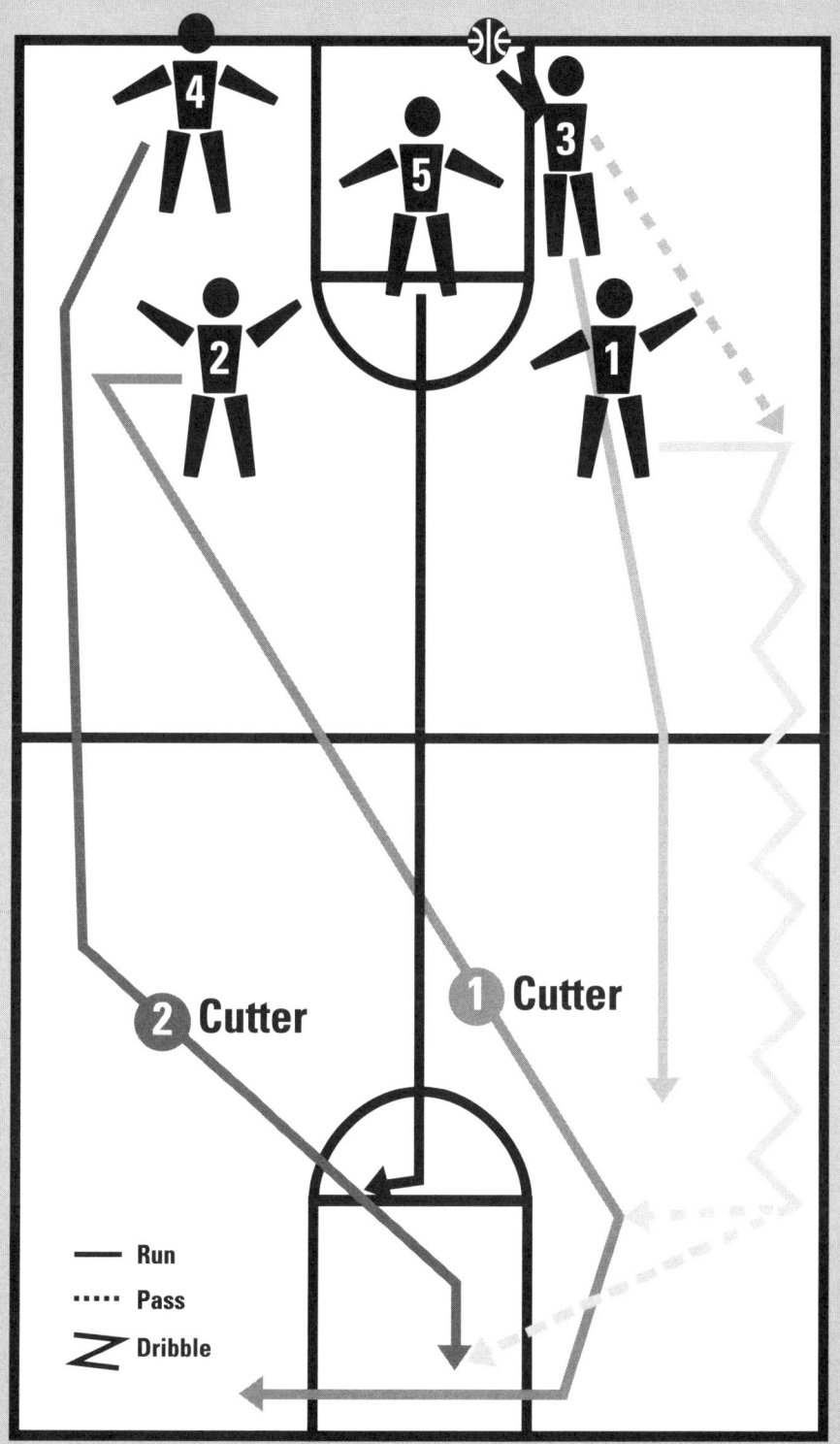

Motion Offense

The motion offense involves continuous movement by all five members of a team, is easy to teach, tough to defend against and enjoyable to coach and play.

- Freedom to Play – Players feel free to create scoring opportunities for themselves and their teammates.
- Easy to Teach – Players at all levels can learn to play motion offense in a short time.
- Flexible – You can attack any defense because you assign each player to a defensive opponent according to size, speed and ability.
- Tough to Defend – Moving players, setting picks, screens, flashes, and backdoor cuts present challenging situations to opponents.
- Matures Players – Continuous repetition of fundamentals in drills designed for motion offense matures players mentally and physically.
- Builds Team Unity – Involves all five players for team's success and enjoyment.

Essential Components

- Passing – Good passing eliminates turnovers and sets up scoring opportunities. Players must work on "passing away from the defense" to ensure the pass receiver not only catches the ball, but is in a position to score.
- Movement – Players should individually, and as a team, maintain good floor balance. It is important to create situations where the opponents have to cover all five players continuously. It should be the goal of each player to "Always move with a purpose."
- Dribbling – The dribble off a fake toward the basket or a screen is used to create a variety of scoring opportunities. The dribbler must always see his teammates, as well as potential defenders
- Screening – The screen is the most effective way of helping your teammates to get good shots. You can have two screening situations going on at the same time. The player with the ball must look for both the player being screened and the screener as potential scoring threats. The best method of screening is for the player to come to a complete stop, have good balance and keep his hands locked. There is less chance of fouling, and the screener gives himself maximum protection.
- Shot Discipline – Motion offense is not a freelance, equal-shot-opportunity game. The discipline of this offense is determined by the types of shots players are permitted to take, plus the number of good shots created for the best scorers on the team.
- Concentration – In pattern offenses, the system does the thinking for the player. In motion offense, the offense will be only as good as the player concentration. This quality is essential in developing a winning team.

Motion Offense

- Role Identification – Roles, rather than positions, are stressed on offense. Each player is to play within his capability. Shot discipline and role identification go together. The coach will assist players to understand their roles and encourage them to do their best.

Basic Principles

- Read the Defense – Each player should take advantage of what his opponent allows. This is called "reading the defense." The offensive player must concentrate on how he is being guarded and the positions of his teammates. He then moves to the best spot to score.

  a. The player without the ball has two basic moves – the V-cut and the screen.

  b. In executing the V-cut, the offensive player takes his defender in one direction, then flashes back toward the potential passer. He jumps to the ball, turns in the air and lands with feet squared toward the basket, which will allow him to take a jump shot or drive either way toward the basket for a lay-up or jumper.

  c. In executing the screen, two players work together to produce a scoring opportunity. The screener first checks to see how his teammate is being defended, then moves to screen his opponent at the best angle, calling out the name of his teammate. The screener then rolls to the basket and opens for the ball or to a rebound position.

  d. Creative movement – Every time down the court on transition, a team should score off the initial or secondary fast break or maintain good floor balance, read the defense and create a scoring opportunity.

  e. Communication – Players must talk continually on both offense and defense. Screeners must call out the name of the players for whom they are screening and alert their teammates of potential screens on defense, as well as point to and call out the number of the player they are defending or switching to take.

1-2-2 Set

G2 down-screens for **F4**;
G3 down-screens for **C5**;
G1 passes to **G3**, who dribbles down the side or passes into **C5**, who shoots

1-2-2 Set

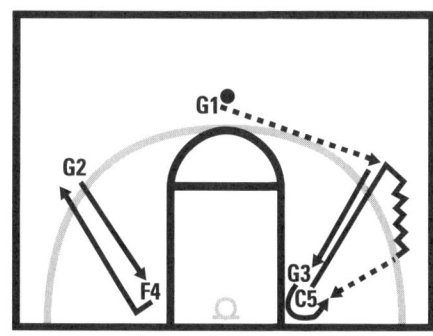

1-2-2 Stack

G2 screens for **F4**, who runs to the right wing position and receives a pass from **G1**;
G3 screens for **C5**, who runs to the right side of the lane and receives a pass from **F4**;
G1 screens for **C5**, who runs to the top of the free throw lane

1-2-2 Stack

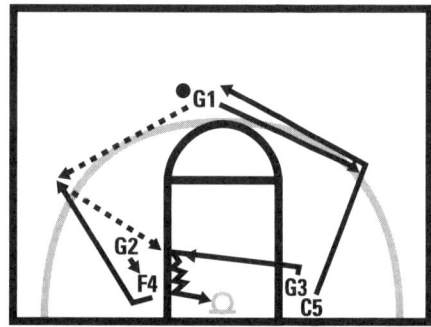

1-3-1 Free Throw Line

G1 passes to **G2**; **C5** cuts to the right side of the lane and receives a pass from **G2**, then dribbles to the basket; **F4** runs to the perimeter and back to rebound; **G3** goes to a rebound position

1-3-1 Free Throw Line

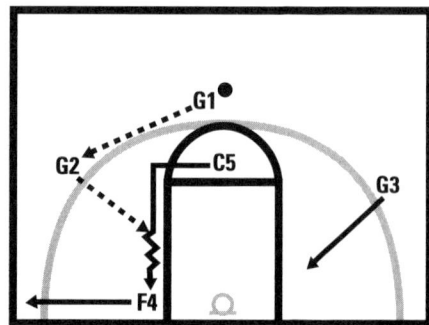

Motion Offense

2-1-2 Set

G1 dribbles to left wing; **G2** runs to replace **G1**; **G3** flashes low across the land and screens for **F4,** who cuts off the screen and runs back door to low post position on opposite side, then flashes to the lane; **G1** looks inside, then reverse passes to **G2**; **G2** passes to **C5** in high post position, who passes low to **F4** for the shot

2-1-2 Set

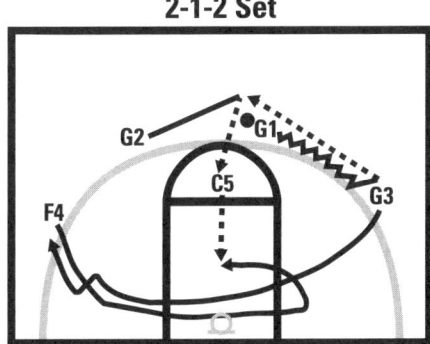

1-3-1 Sequence

G2 dribbles to the point guard position and passes to **G3** on right wing; **G2** runs left to screen for **G1,** who comes to the point guard position; **G3** V-cuts and receives pass from **G2**; **F4** back screens for **C5,** who slides to right side for the pass from **G3** and drives to the basket or takes a jump shot; **F4** flashes back to rebound on the left side

Back Pick for Center

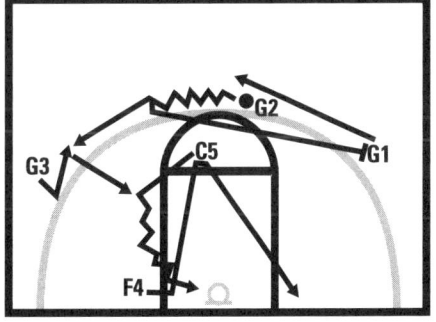

1-2-2 Sequence

G3 and **G2** down screen for **C5** and **F4**; **G1** passes to **C5** on the wing, then screens for **F4,** who assumes the point guard position

Create other options after the initial moves

1-2-2 Free Throw Line

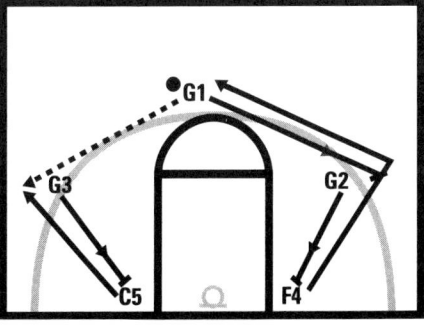

Ten Keys to Playing Defense

1. Accept responsibility for your man.
2. Control the dribbler.
3. Stop penetration.
4. Play denial defense to ball-side, except when trapping the first pass.
5. Be alert to trap and jump situations.
6. Stop the baseline drive and flash.
7. Deny the pass to center, especially the low post.
8. Box out and go for rebounds.
9. Commit yourself to take a charge.
10. Talk on defense.

Basic Rules in Man to Man Defense

- Create a desire and enjoyment for this phase of the game.
- Stay low and anticipate opportunities to strip the ball by scooping. Keep your eyes on the chest of the dribbler. Before attempting to scoop, drop your eye focus to the ball; scoop with the inside hand at the moment the ball leaves the floor, and, if successful, drive to the basket.
- When the dribbler picks up the ball – swarm it.
- Have hand(s) in shooter's face; take away the passing lanes.
- Immediately box out your man when he shoots; then go to the hoop.
- On back pick, automatically switch men; call "Switch," or "I've got 'Number...'"
- Don't switch unless your teammate tells you to on the down pick.
- Defend against the skip pass on the weak side.
- To defend against the give-and-go, chest the cutter; turn away a passing lane
- If your opponent attempts a baseline drive, get your foot out of bounds; force him to drive to the middle of the lane for help.

Defensive Stance

Head and eyes up
Arms and fingers flexed
Bend knees
Up on balls of feet

Defense

- When your post man is taller than you, front or side-saddle; protect the basket.
- On high-post defense, play ball-side; extend your arm into the passing lanes.
- Deny the post from flashing to the ball.
- Force the dribbler to use his weak hand with your body and feet.
- Call "Help" if needed.

Taking a Charge

A player often faces a situation on defense when a quick decision can make a difference in the outcome of the game. Taking a charge can do that. When an offensive player is penetrating the lane and you are defending that area, move quickly to a spot facing him. Plant your feet when he is two or three steps away. Bend both knees slightly and cup your hands down low in front for protection.

On contact with his body, give ground. Drop to a sitting position and bounce right back up.

Basic Man-to-Man Defensive in Relationship to Ball and Floor Position

Man and Ball

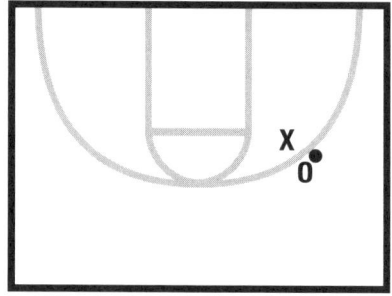

Play even up or half to full step on his dominant hand side

One Pass Away

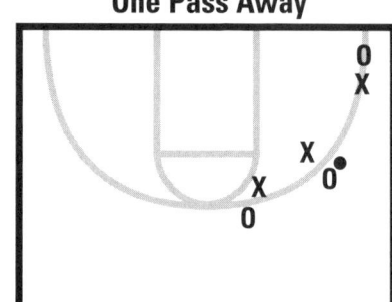

Two Passes Away

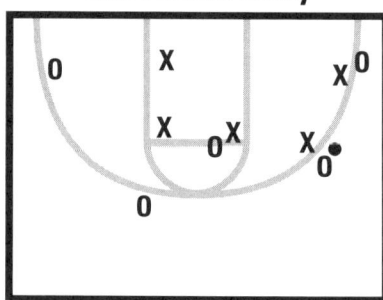

High Post Coverage

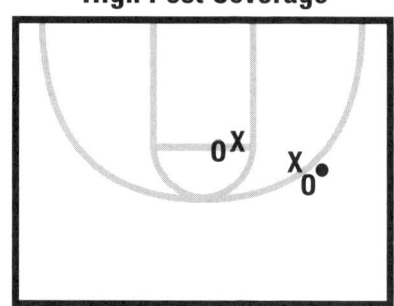

Play ball-side; hand must be in passing lane

Low Post Coverage

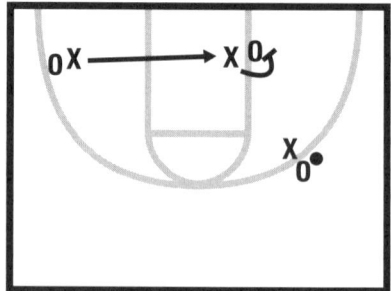

Must front unless given other instructions by Coach; offside help "D" covers the lob pass

5-on-5 Sag to Center Lane

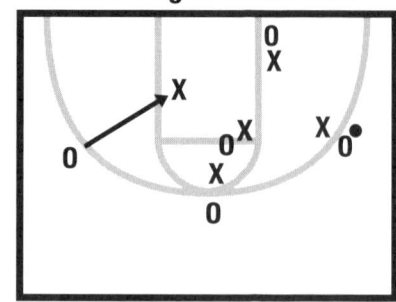

TALK ! TALK! TALK!

Defense

Scramble Defense

- There are variations in codes — numbers, colors, names — to indicate zones or locations. For instance, "22" could mean "apply trap at half court"; "Orange" could mean "full court press"; "Charlie" could mean "run and jump."
- When applying the scramble defense, double up the dribbler or pass receiver with two players. Have two players as intercepters ball-side and one player as a goal tender, opening up under the basket.
- When the ball is reversed away from the trap, one player immediately defenses the pass receiver. Four players scramble to the lane and call out new opponents for straight man-to-man defense.
- Five situations when you scramble out of the zone defense:
    1. Screen on the ball.
    2. Short pass to corner.
    3. Baseline drive.
    4. Pass to low post.
    5. Just behind or over the half-court line when the offensive player advances by dribbling the ball, stops and picks the ball up.

Defense

Zone Press, Box and 1 (20 Red)

G1 deflects attention of the opponent with the ball out of bounds.

G3 denies the pass to his opponent on the opposite side of the court and then slides to the middle after the ball is thrown inbounds.

G2 denies the pass to his opponent on the ballside, who receives the inbounds pass. **G2** then forces the opponent to dribble toward the sideline and gets his own foot out of bounds to force the dribbler to pick up the ball.

F4 plays ballside at half court, denying his opponent. He protects the out of bounds line if **G3** loses his man.

C5 sprints to his own free throw line to defend against any opponent who dribbles or runs to that area. When the ball gets to half-court, each man is responsible for the jersey number he calls out.

Defense

3/4 Trap (30 Blue)

After the ball is passed inbounds, **G3** goes to the opponent with the ball and forces him to the sideline; **G1** sprints to set the trap; **G2** comes to the middle and denies a pass; **F4** sprints to the sideline after he checks other options; **C5** remains on his defensive free throw line

— Run
····· Pass
∽ Dribble

Commitment – the Key

Outstanding athletic performance does not come easily. It requires unrelenting discipline, dedication and commitment. Athletes who win medals pay a high price for such achievements, and many think it's worth it. Yet the act of winning is short-lived, and soon there is another winner and another team that has broken a record.

We should strive to commit to something that will last for eternity. Jesus Christ came to this earth and lived among us. Most people despised Him and didn't want to hear what He had to say. They enjoyed their sin and had no reason to repent. Yet despite all that, He died for each one of us and took our sins upon Himself so that we could have the opportunity, if we choose, to live forever with Him in heaven.

God was in Christ restoring the world to Himself, no longer counting men's sins against them, but blotting them out ...For God took the sinless Christ and poured into Him our sins.
II Corinthians. 5:19, 21

We are all sinners. No one person is perfect, and we will never be perfect, no matter how many times we attend church, help our neighbor, give money to those in need, etc. We are doomed to an eternal hell unless we choose to believe Jesus died for us on that cross, and rose again the third day to be with His Father in heaven.

All have sinned; all fall short of God's standard.
Romans 3:23

Eternal life – it is a free gift from God. It is yours for the asking no matter who you are or where you come from or what you've done or haven't done in your life.

The wages of sin is death, but the free gift of God is eternal life through Jesus Christ our Lord.
Romans 6:23

Just think. If you died tonight, what would happen to you? Where would you end up?

To all who received Him, He gave the right to become children of God. All they needed to do was to trust Him to save them. All those who believe this are reborn; not a physical rebirth resulting from human passion or plan – but from the will of God.
John 1:12,13

Commitment

The Time is Now

Sometimes in the game of basketball you play four quarters, the game ends in a tie and then you play extra minutes to determine a winner. But there is no overtime in life. When it's gone, you're gone, and only you can determine where you will end up. Don't wait!

Where to Begin

Confession – It may seem odd that to be a winner in life, you need to confess failure. Like every other member of the human race, you have fallen short of God's perfect standard, and there is nothing you can do to attain it.

That if you confess with your mouth Jesus as Lord, and believe in your heart that God raised Him from the dead, you shall be saved.
Romans 10:9

Repentance – This is more than simply being sorry for your sin. It means you are willing to turn from sin with the strength God promises to provide.

For whoever will call upon the name of the Lord will be saved.
Romans 10:13

Acceptance – By recognizing that Jesus' death was the price and penalty of your sin, you prepare to receive Him as your personal Lord and Savior. Ask God to forgive your sin and give you new life.

I am the way and the truth and the life; no one comes to the Father but through Me.
John 14:6

Commitment – An athlete's decision to compete does not involve just the game. It includes commitment to the discipline of training. Having asked God for salvation, you must now trust Him for your future.

God has given us eternal life; that life is in His Son. So whoever has God's Son has life; whoever does not have His Son does not have life.
I John 5:11,12

Nothing in this world is more trustworthy than God's Word. He assures us that by accepting Jesus Christ, His Son, we freely receive the eternal life He offers. It begins the moment we trust Him and continues right on to Heaven.

Commitment

A Prayer

You may believe that Jesus is who He says he is, but that belief won't matter in your life until you commit yourself to Him.

Sometimes we don't know where to start, or we think we are not worthy to ask God into our lives. In the Bible, David, who was known as the man after God's own heart, commited unspeakable acts of adultery and murder. Yet God forgave him. No matter what circumstances you find yourself in, God will forgive you.

To become a child of God, you need to sincerely talk to Him. Remember that a prayer to receive Christ is a life-changing decision. If you are ready to make this commitment, the following prayer may be yours:

Dear Jesus,

I confess I am a sinner in your sight and am truly sorry. Please forgive me.

I believe that You died on the cross to pay for my sins and that God raised You from the grave three days later.

I accept You as my substitute and ask You to come into my life and change me so that I will be pleasing to You.

Thank You for forgiving me for my sins, making me a child of God and giving me eternal life with You.

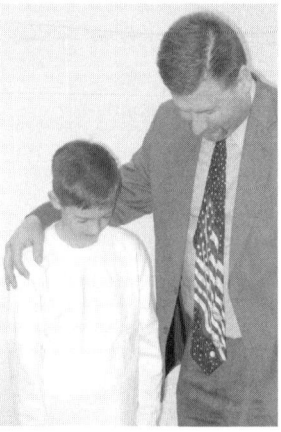

How can I be sure that I have eternal life?

I John 5:1 states, "If you believe that Jesus is the Christ, that He is God's Son and your Savior – then you are a child of God."

The Apostle John goes on to write, *"We believe men who witness in our courts, and so surely we can believe whatever God declares; and God declares that Jesus is His Son. All whoever believe this know in their hearts that it is true. If anyone doesn't believe this, he is actually calling God a liar, because he doesn't believe what God has said about His Son.*

And what is it that God has said? That He has given us eternal life, and that this life is in His Son. So whoever has God's Son has life; whoever does not have His Son does not have life.

I have written this to you who believe in the Son of God so you may know that you have eternal life. And we are sure of this, that He will listen to us whenever we ask Him for anything in line with His will; And if we know He is listening when we talk to Him and make our requests, then we can be sure that He will answer us."

I John 5:9-15

Commitment

Growing in the Lord

Following one's commitment to Christ, here are four additional suggestions that will help you grow and mature in Him:

Prayer — Make prayer a top priority in your daily life. It is as vital to spiritual life as breathing is to physical well being.

Bible Reading — Discover God's direction by reading His Word. Just as you speak to God in prayer, so He speaks to you through the Bible. God cares about every area of your life. His Word addresses each issue you face.

Fellowship — Regular worship with other believers is not only pleasing to God but essential to our spiritual life and ministry to others.

Witnessing — Share with others your decision for Christ and how God has blessed you. Review the scripture verses that were significant to you in coming to Christ, and reach out with the Gospel to others. You will be doubly blessed.

Dear Friend,

How are you? I just had to send you this letter to tell you how much I love you and care about you. I saw you yesterday as you were walking with your friends. I waited all day hoping you would talk to me also.

As evening drew near, I gave you a sunset to close your day and a cool breeze to rest you — And I waited, you never came. Oh! Yes it hurt me, but I still love you because I am your friend.

I saw you fall asleep last night and I longed to touch your brow, so I spilled moonlight upon your pillow and face. Again I waited, wanting to rush down so we could talk. I have so many gifts for you.

You awakened late and rushed off for the day... my tears were in the rain.

Today you looked so sad, so alone. It makes my heart ache because I understand. My friends let me down and hurt me many times too, but I love you. My love for you is deeper than the oceans and bigger than the biggest want or need you have.

We will spend eternity together in heaven. I know how hard it is on this earth. I really know because I was there and I want to help you. My Father wants to help, too, He's that way, you know. Just call me...ask me, talk to me. It is your decision. I have chosen you and because of that I will wait, because I love you.

Your friend, Jesus

About the Author

Wes Shepard

Wes Shepard completed a successful 50-year coaching career in 1999 with a record of 521 wins and 265 losses. His teams made numerous state tournament appearances, winning one championship and four runner-up trophies.

He stepped down from the head coaching position in 2000 to assist one son, Scott, in a successful state championship bid.

Two other sons also were successful coaches. Greg led his team to a state title, and Mark's squad played in the quarterfinals.

Shepard coached high school boys and girls teams in Wisconsin, Illinois and Nebraska. He coached basketball, football, volleyball, and track.

His career also included a football and basketball coaching stint at Luther College which was located in Wahoo, Nebr.

He coached a college all-star team in Europe and a Chinese provincial team in Xian, China.

Throughout his career, the coach built championship programs in each community, working with elementary and junior high athletes to lay a solid foundation of game fundamentals.

Wes Shepard was elected to the Nebraska High School Athletic Hall of Fame in 2002 and the National High School Athletic Coaches Hall of Fame in 2005.

FCA

FCA has made a major impact on our family over the past 40 years.

My wife and I first became involved at the local level in Illinois, where we started huddle groups that met in our home weekly.

I became more active after attending an FCA coaches camp with Tom Landry and Tom Osborne in Kenosha, Wis.

In addition to our huddle meetings, we held Bible studies at the school. More than 300 students and athletes committed their lives to Christ through these activities. We sponsored annual tournaments in our school through FCA, with professional players from Chicago, Milwaukee and Green Bay playing in an all-star basketball game against area coaches and speaking at an outreach breakfast.

Jim Rexillius, football coach at Wheaton North, and I became close friends, and we worked with the Chicago-area FCA office, taking our huddle kids to the Resource Center in Indiana and to camps in Texas and Wisconsin.

Our community had been torn apart by racial rioting in the schools. By working through FCA and area churches, the tensions were overcome within a couple of years, and our schools became models for others in the north Chicago area.

Ron Brown, our state director, has brought a vision for dads to be trained to assume new leadership in their homes and to take responsibility for the athletic and spiritual growth of their sons and daughters.

I would encourage every mom, dad, son and daughter to get involved in the Fellowship of Christian Athletes. It will pay huge dividends in each of your lives for now and eternity.

Basketball Terminology & Symbols

——— Player is running
- - - - - Player is passing
∧∧ Player is dribbling
O   Offensive player
X   Defensive player

Add number for player identification:

Offensive players: O1 (Point Guard); O2 (Guard); O3 (Guard): O4 (Forward); O5 (Center or Forward)

Defensive players: X1; X2; X3; X4; X5

Position by number: Post is same as center

1-2-2 offense	1-3-1 offense
1 - Point guard	1 - Point guard
2 - Right guard	2 - Right guard
3 - Left guard	3 - Left guard
4 - Right forward	4 - Low post
5 - Left forward	5 - High post

Backdoor cut — Offensive player runs low behind the defense to get open for pass.

Breakaway — A player runs or dribbles away from his defender to get into a shooting position..

Charge — Foul for a player who dribbles or runs into an opponent, causing contact.

Drop step — Center or other players who will post up on either side of the lane must step with the foot closest to basket, look over the same shoulder to check the hoop and the defender. If he's open he either pivots to shoot or dribbles to the basket for a lay-up.

Fast break (Primary) (Secondary) — Transition from defense to offense downcourt toward the opponent's basket. Second break to basket if primary break fails to produce score.

Basketball Terminology

Flash or cut	Player sprints to a spot to be able to receive a pass.
Flier or to fly	Player sprints ahead of the opponent to receive a pass to score.
Intensity	A sincere desire for a player to play with all his heart.
Jump to the ball	An offensive player runs toward his teammate with ball, giving the teammate a target with his hands to catch it, yells "Ball," and jumps, landing with feet squared to the basket.
Outlet	A player who runs to an open spot so his teammate can pass to him.
Penetration	To move inside the defense toward the basket with a dribble or cut/flash.
Power-up or rare shot	A player dribbles inside the baseline to the basket, jump-stops with shoulders squared to the board, springs up with the ball held by both hands, then releases the shot off the board.
Pattern	Designed as a play or system of movement that is planned by the coach and put into action by the team members.
Putback or second shot	A shot that follows a rebound of a missed shot.
Scramble	Two or more players sprint to the ball and other opponents to prevent a score.
Set	Players are assigned to certain positions on the court to begin a play, series of plays or creative movement.
Skip Pass	A high pass that is used to get the ball to a teammate in an open position on the other side of the court.
Transition	Team switches from defense to offense or offense to defense.

References

1. DeVenzio, Dick, A Passion for Basketball, Sports Education, Inc., Mars, PA.
2. Farrar, Steve, Finishing Strong, Multnomah Publishers, Inc. Sisters, Oregon
3. Handley, Rod, Character Counts, Cross Training Publishing, Grand Island, NE.
4. Henson, Lou, Myslenski, Skip, Lou Winning at Illinois, Sagamore Publishing, Champaign, Il
5. Neal, Wes, Handbook on Athletic Perfection, Cross Training Publishing, Grand Island, NE.
5. Neal, Wes, Handbook on Coaching Perfection, Cross Training Publishing, Grand Island, NE.
6. Rohrbach, Mike, Denny Rydberg, Run 2 Win, Cross Training Publishing, Grand Island, NE.
7. Schindler, Claude E, Pyle, Pacheco, Sowing for Excellence, ACSI, Whittier, CA.
8. Thornburg, David, The New Basics, ASCD, Alexandria, VA.
9. Winquist, Alan H., Winquist, Jessica Rousselow, Coach Odle's Full Court Press, Taylor University Press, Upland, Ind.
10. Wooden, John, Carty, Jay, Coach Wooden's Pyramid of Success, Gospel Light, Ventura, CA.